CHLOE,
LOVE FROM

Hi, I'm CHLOE! What's your name?

On a normal street like yours and mine,
It was a bright and sunny day.
Chloe opened the door, and suddenly saw,
A gang of animals waiting to play.

The tiger loves taking centre stage,
He's quite the confident one.
But equally, and I'm sure you'll agree,
His shy friends are also fun.

Let'sss play,
CHLOE!

Hide-and-seek's a favourite game,
It's Chloe versus the giraffes.
Her careful disguise won't fool their eyes,
And it ends with smiles and laughs.

Here we come,
CHLOE!

Some friends like to relax and snuggle,
Others creep about and are tickly.
The otters hug, the gorillas are snug,
And the porcupines are cute and prickly.

Wanna hug, CHLOE?

The sloths love hanging out and snoozing,
While the monkeys swing about.
Chloe happily grins at the jumps and spins,
And the wild and cheeky shouts.

Zzzzzz

It's time to settle down for lunch,
Chloe's burger takes some beating.
Her friends have FRUITS,

GRASS, GRUBS and ROOTS,

There's an icky stench wafting
through the air,
And Chloe is turning greener!
It might just be, the hippo, you see,

Or perhaps the RING-TAILED LEMUR?!

Chloe spots the rhinos squabbling,
They're bickering and butting their heads.
She must put a stop, to their childish strop,
"I'll try a spot of juggling," she said.

Chloe's hair is a little bit messy,
"But my friends look much funnier!"
she thinks.

They're **BUSHY** and **BRISTLY**,
SPIKY and **FRIZZY**,
All coloured red, orange
and pinks.

Hooray! They've found a trampoline,
It's sure to raise a grin.

The giraffe takes flight,
And the hippo's a sight,
As they LEAP and

BOUNCE and SPRING.

Night night,
CHLOE

Chloe is ready to head back home,
As night eclipses the day.
But there's still time,
For a little more rhyme,
As her friends have

SOMETHING TO

SAY....

She's fun!
She's clever!
She's friendly!
She's kind!
She really loves to play!

Chloe can't deny,
As she waves goodbye,

Chloe, now draw your different friends and tell us why they're so special.

Written by Joe Barnes
Illustrated by Cinzia Battistel
Designed by Alice Xavier

First published by HOMETOWN WORLD in 2019
Hometown World Ltd
1 Queen Street
Bath
BA1 1HE

Visit
www.hometownworld.co.uk

Follow us @hometownworldbooks

ISBN 978-1-78979-082-5

Printed in Italy
HTW_PO201910

Hometown World